11+
Verbal Reasor
GL & Other Styles

WORKBOOK **1**

Verbal Reasoning Technique

Dr Stephen C Curran
with Jacqui Turner
Edited by Andrea Richardson and Katrina MacKay

This book belongs to

ae PUBLICATIONS
Accelerated Education Publications Ltd

Contents

© 2012 Stephen Curran

Chapter One
ALPHABET REASONING
1. Letter Sequencing

There are six things to look for in **Letter Sequencing**:

a. Basic Sequences	1. Alphabetical Order 2. Forwards and Backwards Movement 3. Leapfrogging
b. Complex Sequences	4. Constant Gaps 5. Increasing or Decreasing Gaps 6. Alternating Gaps

An alphabet is always provided to help with the questions.

a. Basic Sequences

Basic Sequences have three main features:

1. All letter sequences follow **Alphabetical Order**.
2. The sequences can move **Forwards** and **Backwards**.
3. The sequences are established by **Leapfrogging** (jumping over one or more letters).

Example 1: Write the next letter in the sequence:

G P H Q I R ?

- This sequence is alphabetical like all other sequences.
- This sequence has a forwards movement.
- There is leapfrogging. It is necessary to jump over letters to establish the sequence.

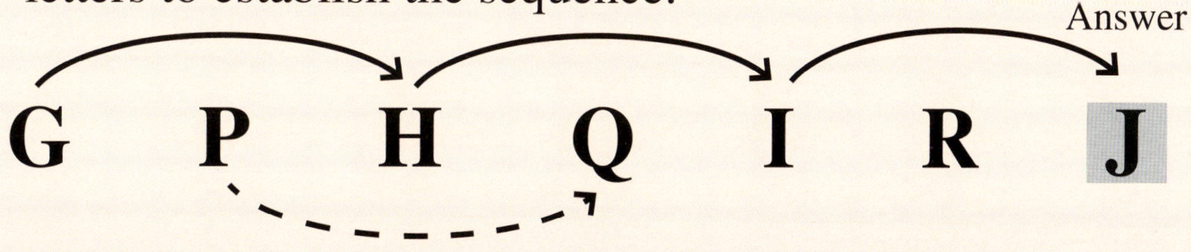

© 2012 Stephen Curran

Example 2: Write the next letter in the sequence:

Q X P Y O Z ?

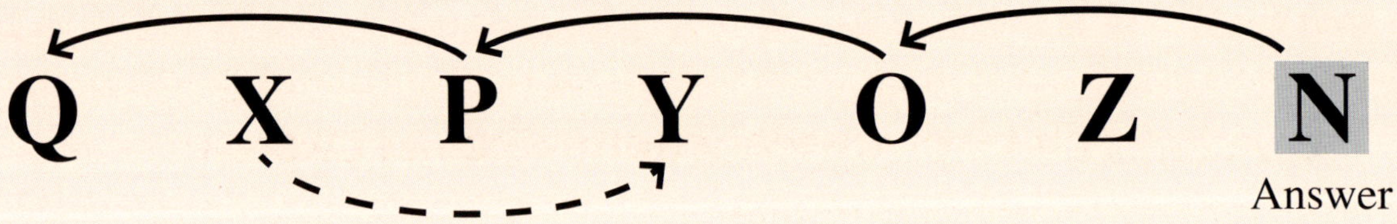

This is an alphabetical, leapfrogging sequence, but there is also a backwards and a forwards movement.

A B C D E F G H I J K L M N O P Q R S T U V W X Y Z

Exercise 1: 1a Write the two missing letters:

1) **AD BE CF DG EH** ______
2) **CD EF GH IJ KL** ______
3) **KZ LY MX NW OV** ______
4) **DE ST FG UV HI** ______
5) **YR ZQ AP BO CN** ______

b. Complex Sequences

4. There can be a **Constant Gap** (or same number of missing letters) between the letters in a sequence. Sequences can be solved either by writing in the missing letters or by counting the gaps between the letters.

Example: Write the next letter in the sequence:

C V E T G R ?

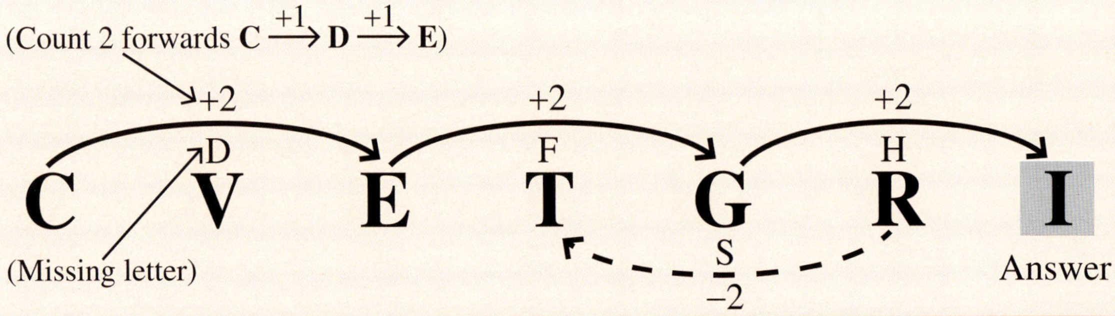

© 2012 Stephen Curran

A plus sign (+) shows forwards movement and a minus sign (–) shows backwards movement.

There is one missing letter between each leapfrogged letter in the forwards movement and one missing letter between each leapfrogged letter in the backwards movement of the sequence.

A B C D E F G H I J K L M N O P Q R S T U V W X Y Z

Exercise 1: 1b Write the two missing letters:

6) **MW OU QS SQ UO** ______

7) **JN KP LR MT NV** ______

8) **DN FL HJ JH LF** ______

9) **PA OY NW MU LS** ______

10) **OA RD UG XJ AM** ______

Record scores out of ten here

5. Sequences often have **Increasing** or **Decreasing** spaces between the letters.

Example:

Write the next letter in the sequence:
D E G J N ?

+1 +2 +3 +4 +5

F HI KLM OPQR

D E G J N S

Answer

This sequence has an increasing number of missing letters in the forwards movement - no missing letters, 1 missing letter, 2 missing letters, etc.

A B C D E F G H I J K L M N O P Q R S T U V W X Y Z

Exercise 1: 2a Write the two missing letters:

1) **KE KF LH NK QO** ______

2) **ZP UK QG ND LB** ______

3) **AB ZC XE UH QL** ______

4) **UC VE XG AI EK** ______

5) **BC DD GF KI PM** ______

6. Sequences often have **Alternating Gaps** between the letters.

Example: Write the next letter in the sequence:
L N N Q Q S S V ?

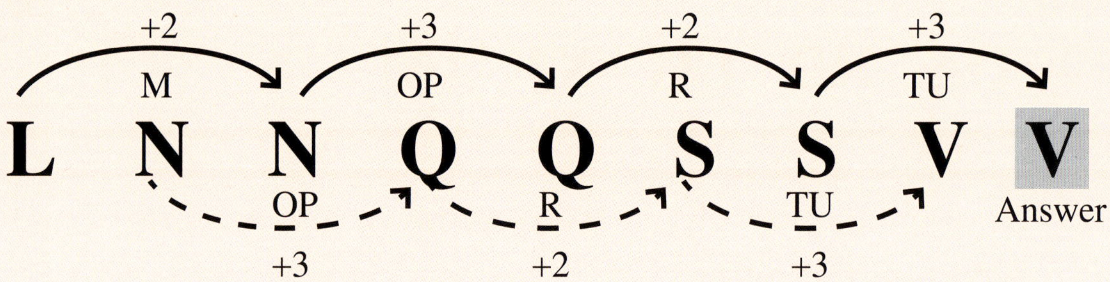

This sequence alternates between 1 missing letter and 2 missing letters in a forwards leapfrogging movement.

Letter sequences can have multiple solutions. For example, this sequence also alternates between a forwards movement alternating gap and a repeated letter.

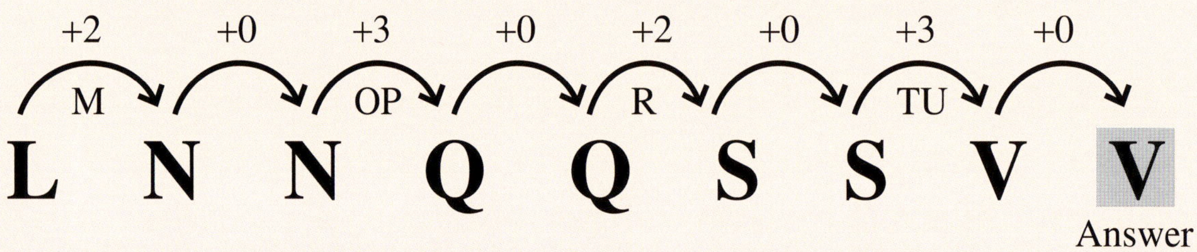

© 2012 Stephen Curran

A B C D E F G H I J K L M N O P Q R S T U V W X Y Z

Exercise 1: 2b Write the two missing letters:

6) **AB CD DF FH GJ** ______

7) **NP MO JL IK FH** ______

8) **SJ VI YG BF ED** ______

9) **GR GT HV HX IZ** ______

10) **HI JK KL MN NO** ______

c. *Mixed Examples*

Exercise 1: 3 Write the two missing letters:

1) **MZ OX QV ST UR** ______

2) **AB YZ CD WX EF** ______

3) **RA RC QE QG PI** ______

4) **LP MO OM RJ VF** ______

5) **DU GS JQ MO PM** ______

6) **KR MT NU PW QX** ______

7) **WK TJ SI PH OG** ______

8) **CS DT EU FV GW** ______

9) **EF HI KL NO QR** ______

10) **PQ RS TU VW XY** ______

© 2012 Stephen Curran

2. Alphabet Codes

An alphabet is always provided to help with the questions. There are two basic categories of **Alphabet Codes**:

a. Plus and Minus Codes a) Letter to Letter Code
b) Word to Code
c) Code to Word

b. Position Codes (by counting position in the alphabet)

a. Plus and Minus Codes

a) **Letter to Letter Code**

This is the simplest type of **Plus and Minus Code**. A Letter to Letter relationship is established with either a forwards or backwards movement in the alphabet.

Example: Write the missing letters:
HC is to **KX** as **YP** is to **?**

1. The alphabet is given and gaps between the letters are counted forwards and backwards to give the code.

– (backwards) + (forwards)

A B C D E F G H I J K L M N O P Q R S T U V W X Y Z

– The next backwards letter would be **Z**.

The next forwards letter would be **A**. +

2. Movement 1 (**H** to **K**) is a forwards movement of **Plus 3** on the alphabet (count the gaps and not the letters).

+3

F G **H** I J **K** L M

3. Movement 2 (**C** to **X**) is a backwards movement of **Minus 5** on the alphabet.

–5

W **X** Y Z A B **C** D

© 2012 Stephen Curran

4. This movement can be shown on the following grid:

+3	–5	
H	**C**	is to **KX**

5. Movements 1 and 2 are now applied to the letters **YP**.

+3	–5	
Y	**P**	is to ?

6. Apply the forwards movement of **Plus 3** to the letter **Y**.

+3

V W X Y Z A B C

Answer is **B**

7. Apply the backwards movement of **Minus 5** to the letter **P**.

–5

J K L M N O P Q

Answer is **K**

The answer is: **BK**

A B C D E F G H I J K L M N O P Q R S T U V W X Y Z

Exercise 1: 4a Write the missing letters:

Score

1) **DE** is to **HI** as **RS** is to **?** ______

2) **IR** is to **LW** as **DT** is to **?** ______

3) **AO** is to **YM** as **CQ** is to **?** ______

4) **XY** is to **RU** as **JK** is to **?** ______

5) **PL** is to **SI** as **NH** is to **?** ______

© 2012 Stephen Curran

b) **Word to Code**

This is the second type of Plus and Minus Code. A Word to Code relationship is established again with either a forwards or backwards movement in the alphabet. The same rules apply except that words are used, which permit longer and more complex codes.

Example: If the code for **CAT** is **FCW**, what is the code for **DOG**?

1. Work out the code by counting the gaps forwards or backwards on the alphabet. This word to code relationship only counts forwards.

Backwards − ← | → **Forwards** +

A B C D E F G H I J K L M N O P Q R S T U V W X Y Z

C +3 → and so on

2. The movement can be shown on the following grid:

+3	+2	+3
C	**A**	**T**

will give: **FCW**

3. The grid and alphabet can now be used to create the new code.

Backwards − ← | → **Forwards** +

A B C D E F G H I J K L M N O P Q R S T U V W X Y Z

D +3 → and so on

+3	+2	+3
D	**O**	**G**

will give the answer: **GQJ**

© 2012 Stephen Curran

A B C D E F G H I J K L M N O P Q R S T U V W X Y Z

Exercise 1: 4b Write the missing code:

6) If the code for **BACK** is **DCEM**,
what is the code for **THEM**? __________

7) If the code for **STONE** is **TVRRJ**,
what is the code for **ROCKS**? __________

8) If the code for **BLINK** is **ZJGLI**,
what is the code for **WINKS**? __________

9) If the code for **TRACK** is **SPXYF**,
what is the code for **RAILS**? __________

10) If the code for **PROVE** is **PTOXE**,
what is the code for **ALLOW**? __________

c) **Code to Word**

This is the third type of Plus and Minus Code. This time a Code to Word relationship is established with either a forwards or backwards movement in the alphabet.

There is one major difference; all Code to Word types require a **reversal of the original forwards or backwards movement** to create the word.

Example: If the code for **RUN** is **OSM**, what does **GMF** stand for?

1. Work out the code on the alphabet as before by counting forwards or backwards. This code counts backwards.

Backwards − ← → + **Forwards**

A B C D E F G H I J K L M N O P Q R S T U V W X Y Z

−3 and so on

2. The movement can be shown on the following grid:

OSM ←

−3	−2	−1
R	**U**	**N**

3. The grid and alphabet can now be used to create the new word. It must be **reversed** because we have to go back to a word from a code.

Backwards − ← → + **Forwards**

A B C D E F G H I J K L M N O P Q R S T U V W X Y Z

+3 and so on

+3	+2	+1
G	**M**	**F**

→ **JOG**

Answer

A B C D E F G H I J K L M N O P Q R S T U V W X Y Z

Exercise 1: 5a Write the missing letters:

1) If the code for **DOG** is **FQI**,
what does **NCR** stand for? ____________

© 2012 Stephen Curran

A B C D E F G H I J K L M N O P Q R S T U V W X Y Z

2) If the code for **MAY** is **JXV**,
what does **IBQ** stand for? __________

3) If the code for **NOT** is **OQW**,
what does **XCJ** stand for? __________

4) If the code for **CAR** is **CBT**,
what does **VBP** stand for? __________

5) If the code for **TEA** is **SCX**,
what does **BSM** stand for? __________

b. Position (Mirror) Codes

Position or **Mirror Codes** can easily be confused with Plus and Minus Codes as the questions are set out in an identical way.

Example: If the code for **HEM** is **SVN**, what is the code for **TOY**?

a. Position or Mirror Codes are created by reflecting a word or code from one half of the alphabet to the other.

b. The alphabet has 26 letters. If it is divided into two halves there will be 13 letters on each side.

13 letters from A to M	**13 letters from N to Z**
A B C D E F G H I J K L M	**N O P Q R S T U V W X Y Z**

1. **HEM** is created by counting from the nearest point to either end of the first half of the alphabet. **H** count left 6; **E** count right 5; **M** count left 1 letter(s).

2. **SVN** is a mirror reflection on the other side of the alphabet. **S** count right 6; **V** count left 5; **N** count right 1 letter(s).

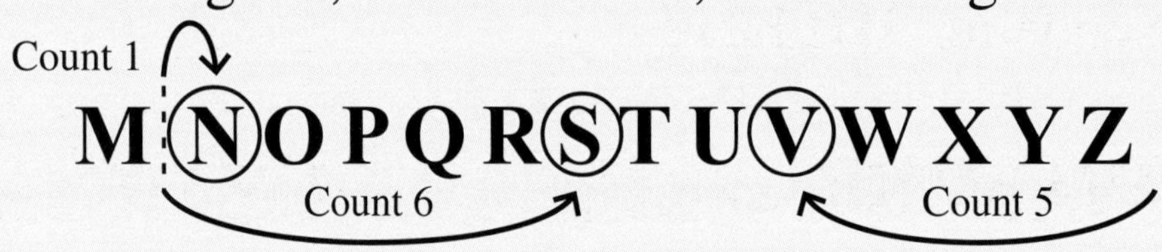

3. If we now view the whole alphabet we can see the reflection, or mirror effect, of the word and the code.

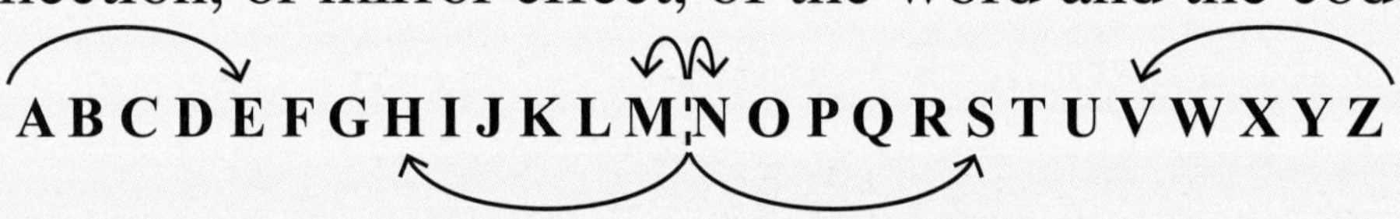

To find the new code we repeat the same mirroring process.

4. **TOY** is created in the same way as above. **T** count right 7; **O** count right 2; **Y** count left 2 letters.

5. Now we can create the missing code. **G** count left 7; **L** count left 2; **B** count right 2 letters.

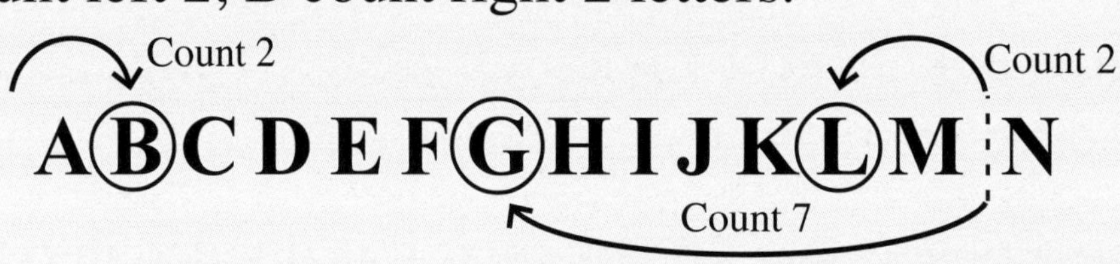

6. The word **TOY** is reflected to make the code **GLB**.

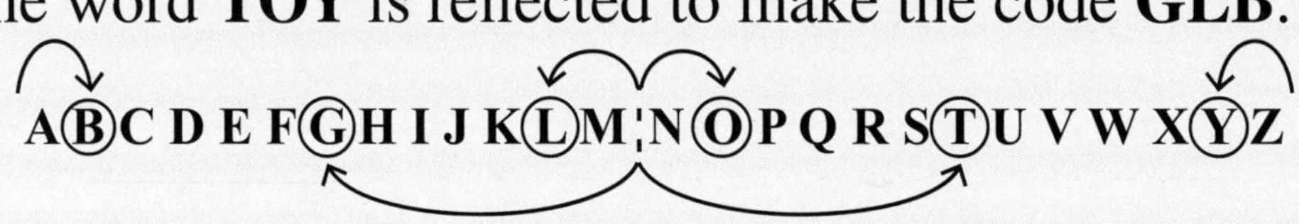

The answer is: **GLB**

© 2012 Stephen Curran

A B C D E F G H I J K L M N O P Q R S T U V W X Y Z

Exercise 1: 5b Write the missing letters:

6) If the code for **LAMP** is **OZNK**, what is the code for **BULB**? __________

7) If the code for **WASP** is **DZHK**, what is the code for **BEES**? __________

8) If **WANTS** is written in code as **DZMGH**, what is the code for **NEEDS**? __________

9) If the code for **PLAY** is **KOZB**, what is the code for **WORK**? __________

10) If **BOAT** is written in code as **YLZG**, what is the code for **FISH**? __________

Score

c. Mixed Examples

A B C D E F G H I J K L M N O P Q R S T U V W X Y Z

Exercise 1: 6 Write the missing letters:

Score

1) a) **BD** is to **DF** as **RV** is to **?** ________

b) **NO** is to **KL** as **UV** is to **?** ________

2) a) **AE** is to **FJ** as **KO** is to **?** ________

b) **VZ** is to **QU** as **YC** is to **?** ________

A B C D E F G H I J K L M N O P Q R S T U V W X Y Z

3) a) **FG** is to **HE** as **OP** is to **?** ________

b) **DE** is to **BH** as **TU** is to **?** ________

4) a) **AB** is to **FW** as **DE** is to **?** ________

b) **WX** is to **YV** as **QR** is to **?** ________

5) a) **RS** is to **VW** as **IS** is to **?** ________

b) **PQ** is to **TM** as **NO** is to **?** ________

6) If the code for **WRONG** is **UPMLE**, what is the code for **RIGHT**? __________

7) If the code for **HORSE** is **SLIHV**, what is the code for **PONIES**? __________

8) If **LETTER** in code is **MGWXJX**, what is the code for **BOOKS**? __________

9) If the code for **FILMS** is **EGIIN**, what is the code for **PLAYS**? __________

10) If the code for **DRUMS** is **WIFNH**, what is the code for **PIANO**? __________

© 2012 Stephen Curran

Chapter Two
WORD PATTERNS and CODES

1. Word Patterns

Word Pattern questions involve the use of numbering to discover one new word from a given word or words.
There are two types of question:

a. Finding a missing word from a **One Word Pattern**.
b. Finding a missing word from a **Two Word Pattern**.

a. One Word Pattern

In **One Word Pattern** questions, two pairs of words are given. The missing word is found by applying the number pattern that links the word pairs.

Example: Find the missing word:

(relied deer) (larger real)
(mallet ?)

1. Number the first word. The letters are now represented by numbers. Number the second word accordingly.

1 2 3 4 5 6	6 2 5 1 (5 2)
relied	**deer**

2. Number the second pair of words to clarify which letters should be chosen to make the correct pattern.

1 2 3 4 5 6	6 5 2 1
larger	**real**

3. Number the word in the third grouping and repeat the number pattern to find the missing word.

1 2 3 4 5 6 — **mallet**

6 5 2 1 — **?**

4. Now create the new word by using the pattern.

6 5 2 1

Answer: **team**

Exercise 2: 1 Fill in the missing word:

Score

1) **(pace ape) (race are)**
(rice ?) ____________

2) **(gram ram) (grim rim)**
(plot ?) ____________

3) **(glide lid) (blade lad)**
(sled ?) ____________

4) **(crazy cry) (trendy try)**
(pound ?) ____________

5) **(wants swan) (roped drop)**
(hopes ?) ____________

6) **(chimp chip) (short shot)**
(clout ?) ____________

© 2012 Stephen Curran

7) **(blonde bone) (pounds puns)**
(fringe ?) __________

8) **(barrier rear) (rampart trap)**
(toenail ?) __________

9) **(streams seat) (bureaux beau)**
(dewater ?) __________

10) **(drill lid) (trade eat)**
(beast ?) __________

b. Two Word Pattern

In **Two Word Pattern** questions, two sets of words are given. The middle word of the first set has been made from the outer two words. The middle word of the second set must be found.

Example:

Find the missing word:
(garage [goat] lottery) (sorrow [?] staple)

1. Number the middle word of the first set of words in numerical order.

1 2 3 4
(garage [goat] lottery)

2. Using the numbers from the middle word, number each of the common letters from the two words either side.

1 3 3 1 1 2 3 4 2 4 4
(garage [goat] lottery)

3. Number the second set of outer words in the same way.

(sorrow [   ] staple)

sorrow: s = 1, r = 3, r = 3, o = 1 — [1 2 3 4] — staple: t = 2, p = 4, l = 4

4. Number the missing space and write the various alternatives from the outer words below it.

(sorrow [   ] staple)

sorrow: s = 1, r = 3, r = 3, o = 1 — [1 2 3 4] — staple: t = 2, p = 4, l = 4

s t o a
o   r p

5. Write in the letters where there are no choices.

1 2 3 4

[t   ]

s t o a
o   r p

6. Select the correct letters to create the missing word. There is only ever one correct answer.

Answer: **[s t o p]**

Exercise 2: 2 Fill in the missing word:

Score

1) **(sand [fade] face) (sofa [______] sour)**

2) **(stew [flew] leaf) (feta [______] over)**

3) **(heat [boat] above) (rate [______] plait)**

© 2012 Stephen Curran

4) **(left [gift] right)** **(book [______] socks)**

5) **(first [star] faces)** **(cargo [______] guilt)**

6) **(fried [fold] mould)** **(twice [______] taupe)**

7) **(cater [ate] apple)** **(drink [______] cling)**

8) **(letter [reed] pound)** **(jacket [______] diner)**

9) **(pencil [prune] ruler)** **(candy [______] raved)**

10) **(nearby [born] factory)** **(kettle [______] ceiling)**

2. Secret Code

In **Secret Code** questions some codes and words are given. The codes are not written in the same order as the words and one word or code can be irrelevant to the question.

Example: Find the correct code for each word.

BAR	**TAN**	**ARC**	**CAT**
568	**456**	**857**	

As a starting point look for:
Letter(s) in the same position in two or more words.
Letter(s) at the opposing ends of two or more words.

1. Letter **A** is in the same position in **BAR**, **TAN** and **CAT**.
   Letter **T** begins **TAN** and ends **CAT**.
   Letter **C** begins **CAT** and ends **ARC**.

© 2012 Stephen Curran

2. **BAR** and **ARC** are linked together as **AR** are in the same order in both words. **AR** must be **56** as these numbers occur twice in the codes.

	4 5 6	**5 6 8**
Answer:	**BAR**	**ARC**

3. **CAT** and **TAN** are linked together because they both have the letters **A** and **T**. **TAN** cannot be the correct word because there is no code number for **N**.

4. We know from **ARC** that **C** is **8**. Therefore **CAT** must be **857**.

	8 5 7
Answer:	**CAT**

Exercise 2: 3 Find the answers to the following:

START	**CHART**	**STARS**	**PARTS**
63421	**12341**	**57342**	**12342**

1) Find the code for the word **PATCH**. __________
2) Find the code for the word **TRAPS**. __________
3) Find the code for the word **CHAPS**. __________
4) Which word has the code **53421**? __________
5) Which word has the code **53257**? __________

PROVE	**GROOVE**	**GROVE**	**GRAVE**
12457	**62357**	**123357**	**12357**

6) Find the code for the word **VERGE**. __________

© 2012 Stephen Curran

7) Find the code for the word **RAVER.** ___________

8) Find the code for the word **GRAPE.** ___________

9) Which word has the code **6772**? ___________

10) Which word has the code **41277**? ___________

Score

3. Mixed Examples

Exercise 2: 4 Answer the following:

Score

1) **(garner earn) (hoarse soar)**
(master ?) ___________

2) **(mantras tram) (depress reed)**
(lantern ?) ___________

3) **(boomed mood) (flambé male)**
(plague ?) ___________

4) **(winch [chip] snips) (least [_____] drape)**

5) **(barge [crab] coach) (balls [_____] spire)**

6) **(storm [must] sound) (steam [_____] bland)**

SPOON	SCONES	CONES	CLOSE
14332	57316	153261	53261

7) Find the code for the word **LOOSE.** ___________

8) Find the code for the word **COLON.** ___________

9) Which word has the code **57326**? ___________

10) Which word has the code **17346**? ___________

Chapter Three
VOCABULARY with SPELLING

These techniques require basic spelling skills and the ability to recognise words (but not necessarily their meaning).

1. Letter Shift

In **Letter Shift** questions one letter is moved from the first word to the second word, to make two new words. No other rearrangement takes place and the new words make sense.

Example: Move one letter from the first word to the second word to make two new words from:
CRAVE and **COW**

1. Try removing each letter at a time from the first word to see what new words can be made:

   CRAVE The **C** can be removed to make **RAVE**.
   The **R** can be removed to make **CAVE**.

2. Test which letter can be placed in the second word by spreading out the letters so there is space to try out the possibilities. The **C** will not fit into the word anywhere, but the **R** will fit into the second word.

   C~~R~~AVE and **C R O W**

3. Write out the two new words:

   CAVE and **CROW**

© 2012 Stephen Curran

Exercise 3: 1 Answer the following:

Score

1) **GLADE** and **MAN** become ________ and ________

2) **PLANT** and **RAP** become ________ and ________

3) **GLOAT** and **COVE** become ________ and ________

4) **GRAVE** and **CHAT** become ________ and ________

5) **CREATE** and **BARD** become ________ and ________

6) **LEAPT** and **ABLE** become ________ and ________

7) **ROVES** and **NETS** become ________ and ________

8) **TREND** and **LEAN** become ________ and ________

9) **PRAISED** and **LAID** become ________ and ________

10) **PLAYER** and **RISE** become ________ and ________

2. Compound Word

In **Compound Word** questions it is necessary to find two words, one from each group, that together make one correctly spelt word without changing the order of the letters. The word from the first group always comes first.

Example:

Combine two words to make a compound word.	**(at head long)** **(ring rest home)**

If a quick scan of the words does not give the answer, try writing out the nine possibilities. The two words placed together will often trigger the correct answer.

© 2012 Stephen Curran

atring atrest athome headring **headrest**
headhome longring longrest longhome

'headring' looks like a word but it is not in the dictionary. None of the other combinations gives recognisable words. The only real possibility is **'headrest'** and this is a word.

The answer is: **head rest** (the word is **headrest**).

Exercise 3: 2 Write the compound word:

Score

1) **(good life hand)**
(time thing death)

____

2) **(flat ham hand)**
(mock pack land)

____

3) **(real too any)**
(body large other)

____

4) **(butter flat gain)**
(cap time cup)

____

5) **(gold pram mast)**
(fish gain chip)

____

6) **(heel leg foot)**
(long print toe)

____

7) **(grace black boast)**
(bored board full)

____

8) **(bad rail car)**
(road train horn)

____

9) **(cape fast ring)**
(let pull stop)

____

10) **(care wind much)**
(less ring pets)

____

© 2012 Stephen Curran

Many compound words are **elisions** of two words. This means there is a change of sound when the words merge.

Example:

Combine two words to make a compound word.	**(gad toe rib)** **(gone get tell)**

The answer is: **gad get** (the word is **gadget**).

As separate words, **gad** and **get** sound different from when they are merged together as **gadget**. The **d** and **g** make a **j** sound when elided.

Exercise 3: 3 Write the compound word:

Score

1) **(met poor mind)**
   (able lay hod)

   ____

2) **(prime pan pant)**
   (time try lent)

   ____

3) **(grow link bored)**
   (less age robe)

   ____

4) **(inner orb enter)**
   (it note room)

   ____

5) **(back waist clip)**
   (coat card pain)

   ____

6) **(plan band poor)**
   (net age lay)

   ____

7) **(grim flat meat)**
   (fish wall ace)

   ____

8) **(stay hand hear)**
   (some ache wear)

   ____

9) **(high know pact)**
   (wire chin ledge)

   ____

10) **(rat miss hair)**
    (age trip her)

    ____

3. Hidden Word

In these sentences, a **Hidden Word** of four letters must be found at the end of one word and the beginning of the next word.

Example: Find the hidden four-letter word in the sentence:
Nobody should look after your gear.

1. Scan the line looking carefully at the beginning and end of words to see if you can spot the word immediately.
2. If this does not work, use the following technique:

Using your thumbs, cover four letters at the beginning and end of words. When working across two words there are three possibilities. **In multiple-choice papers this technique can be applied directly on the answer sheet.** In this example, these two words hold the answer.

3 - 1	2 - 2	1 - 3
y**our g**ear	yo**ur ge**ar	you**r gea**r
ourg is not a word.	**urge** is a word.	**rgea** is not a word.

The answer is: **urge** (yo**ur ge**ar)

Exercise 3: 4 Write the four-letter word:
(The questions are printed larger to enable you to practise your technique.)

Score

1) There was no way out of the burning building. ______
2) The chimp lay down on the straw. ______
3) The children tried to climb the tree. ______

© 2012 Stephen Curran

4) He was praised for his efforts. ______

5) It was very scenic rowing down the river. ______

6) The film star was rich and famous. ______

7) He bought an ice cream from the shop. ______

8) The climb up the hill was very arduous. ______

9) Having rambled for hours the walkers were extremely tired. ______

10) The assault course was our biggest challenge. ______

4. Missing Letters

a. Type 1

In the first type of **Missing Letter** question, the same letter must fit into both sets of brackets to complete the word in front of the brackets and begin the word after the brackets.

Example:

Find the missing letter that completes all four words.	**ree [?] oan** **fow [?] obe**

1. Go through the alphabet. Is it **a**? Is it **b**? etc. and try out these letters in the spaces in a standard test.
2. **Note that multiple-choice tests give five alternatives, so these can immediately be tried out in the spaces.**

The missing letter is **l**

ree [l] oan
fow [l] obe

The four words are: **reel loan fowl lobe**

Exercise 3: 5 Fill in the missing letter:

Score

1) **chi [?] ort**
cha [?] int
The letter is ____.

2) **las [?] rip**
par [?] own
The letter is ____.

3) **grai [?] ail**
plai [?] est
The letter is ____.

4) **sno [?] orn**
gro [?] aist
The letter is ____.

5) **pla [?] awn**
awa [?] acht
The letter is ____.

6) **blac [?] nife**
por [?] neel
The letter is ____.

7) **brin [?] lade**
kin [?] naw
The letter is ____.

8) **chin [?] corn**
who [?] gain
The letter is ____.

9) **gra [?] ast**
plu [?] ite
The letter is ____.

10) **cub [?] asy**
din [?] ast
The letter is ____.

© 2012 Stephen Curran

b. Type 2

In the second type of **Missing Letter** question, the same letter must fit into all of the sets of brackets to complete each of the two, three or four words.

Example: Find the missing letter that completes all four words.

(_)ven   s(_)uth   als(_)   err(_)r

1. Examine all four words, as the missing letter might be apparent straight away.

2. Test out letters from the alphabet. Is it **a**? Is it **b**? etc. and try out these letters in the spaces provided.

3. **If it is a multiple-choice test that provides five alternatives, these letters can immediately be tried out in the spaces.**

The missing letter is **o**

(o)ven   s(o)uth   als(o)   err(o)r

The four words are:

oven   south   also   error

Exercise 3: 6 Fill in the missing letter:

Score

1) **fl(_)(_)ce   (_)agl(_)**

The letter is ____.

2) **m(_)t(_)r ch(_)(_)se**

The letter is ____.

3) **(_)o(_)(_)y chea(_)**

The letter is ____.

4) **pu(_)(_)le qui(_) (_)ero**

The letter is ____.

5) **(_)lt(_)r extr(_) d(_)wn**

The letter is ____.

6) **g(_)ance (_)ove(_)y came(_)**

The letter is ____.

7) **blo(_) (_)oman t(_)in (_)histle**

The letter is ____.

8) **(_)art terrifi(_) es(_)ape pit(_)h**

The letter is ____.

9) **almo(_)t (_)cale wi(_)e pea(_)**

The letter is ____.

10) **wh(_)le (_)sland adv(_)ce yet(_)**

The letter is ____.

© 2012 Stephen Curran

5. Scrambled Words

In these question types, two words in a sentence have been scrambled. These two words each have one letter missing and they are both missing the same letter.

Example: Find the letter that will complete both of the scrambled words in the sentence below.

My mtero works as a ecf.

Five possibilities are given in the answers section:

t o r h s

1. Read the sentence carefully and think of the context. This may identify the scrambled words immediately.

   This sentence is about work.
   A job someone can have is a chef.
   'My' implies a relation. My mother could work as a chef.

   If this does not work move on to step 2.

2. Add each of the five possible missing letters in turn to try and unscramble m, t, e, r, o and e, c, f.

   For example, the combinations of e, c, f + **t** will not form any words, e.g. ecft, efct, efct, etc.

   However, the combination of e, c, f + **h** will form the word **chef**, and m, t, e, r, o + **h** will form the word **mother**.

3. This forms the sentence:

   My **mother** works as a **chef**.

   Both words are missing the letter **h**.

   The missing letter is: **h**

Exercise 3: 7

Find the letter that will complete both of the scrambled words in the sentence:

Score

1) omts often fly towards the glit

   The five possibilities are: h r w s y ______

2) Jenny's favourite clruo is egran.

   The five possibilities are: i u r a o ______

3) The receipt showed the ecri he dai.

   The five possibilities are: p s l t n ______

4) The anwes has been marked as cretoc.

   The five possibilities are: s f t r c ______

5) She is nlganre how to wms.

   The five possibilities are: u e a i o ______

6) Jessie went ice tisgnk with her fimly.

   The five possibilities are: u e a o i ______

7) We went to the eiadse when it was ynnu.

   The five possibilities are: r t v s h ______

8) His tryo is about a superhero ngvia the world.

   The five possibilities are: r s h c g ______

9) Insects include eesetl, sfreilttue and ants.

   The five possibilities are: l b r g f ______

10) The books are rve thick and eavh.

    The five possibilities are: i y e o a ______

© 2012 Stephen Curran

6. Mixed Examples

Exercise 3: 8

Score

Move one letter to make two new words:

1) **FRONT** and **AMP** become ________ and ________

2) **CHIMP** and **ALL** become ________ and ________

Join two words to make a compound word:

3) **(star tars slip)**
(trip chin light)

____

4) **(stop nest book)**
(bird let dogs)

____

Find the hidden four-letter word in the sentence:

5) Their mountain climb was slow and difficult.

____

6) It was cold and snowy last winter. _________

Find the missing letter that completes all four words:

7) **firs [?] ram**
las [?] rack

The letter is ___.

8) **ca(_)(_)ot (_)oto(_)**

The letter is ___.

Find the letter that will complete both of the scrambled words in the sentence:

9) The manw is talking on the ephn.
The five possibilities are: a e i o u ______

10) The highlighter is tbrih eenr.
The five possibilities are: s g c t k ______

© 2012 Stephen Curran

Chapter Four
VOCABULARY with MEANING

These techniques require an ability to recognise words and understand their meaning within the context of a sentence. Good spelling skills help this recognition process, but many children can read and understand words they cannot spell.

1. Analogy

An **Analogy** is a similarity in meaning between two parallel statements or words. This comparison is linked by the word 'as' which means 'like'.

Example:

Write the word that will complete the analogy.	**Cheer** is to catcall as **applaud** is to (show boo clap)

1. Read the possibilities carefully and try and identify the basis of comparison. Here the basis of similarity between the two statements is signs of audience response.

2. Having decided the basis of comparison, try each option to find the analogy that works best.

The correct answer is boo. It should read:
Cheer is to **catcall** as **applaud** is to **boo**

© 2012 Stephen Curran

Exercise 4: 1

Write the word that will complete the analogy:

Score

1) **Up** is to **down**
as **dim** is to
(wrong left bright)

____

2) **Ear** is to **hear**
as **eye** is to
(sight see look)

____

3) **Love** is to **hate**
as **laugh** is to
(try cry giggle)

____

4) **Boat** is to **sail**
as **plane** is to
(fly flight sky)

____

5) **Summer** is to **hot**
as **winter** is to
(cold snow rain)

____

6) **Four** is to **eight**
as **six** is to
(three twelve sixteen)

____

7) **Cat** is to **kitten**
as **dog** is to
(bark puppy walk)

____

8) **Part** is to **trap**
as **snip** is to
(snap port pins)

____

9) **Finger** is to **hand**
as **toe** is to
(foot boot shoe)

____

10) **Bring** is to brought
as **fight** is to
(fright fought court)

____

© 2012 Stephen Curran

2. Similar Meanings (Synonyms)

In these questions it is necessary to find two words, one from each group, that are most **Similar in Meaning**.

Example: Which two words are similar in meaning?

(peaceful war destroy)
(pain love feud)

1. Scan both sets of words to see if you can spot the answer immediately. If this does not work move on to step 2.
2. Compare each of the nine possibilities:
   peaceful - pain; peaceful - love; peaceful - feud
   war - pain; war - love; **war - feud**
   destroy - pain; destroy - love; destroy - feud
3. Test the words in a sentence: 'A **war** broke out' and 'A **feud** broke out'. They should be the same part of speech and convey the same meaning.

The correct answer is: **war - feud**

Exercise 4: 2

Write the two words closest in meaning:

Score

1) (sand bucket flag)
   (pail spade bag)
   __________ __________

2) (bread slice cheese)
   (pickle roll butter)
   __________ __________

3) (stalk root leaf)
   (stem follow tall)
   __________ __________

4) (jump run stamp)
   (walk hop stroll)
   __________ __________

5) (neck shoulder brow)
   (nose cheek throat)
   __________ __________

6) (break brake drop)
   (fix smash rise)
   __________ __________

© 2012 Stephen Curran

7) (woman toddler man)
(lady girl child)

__________ __________

8) (toddle fly run)
(race jog swim)

__________ __________

9) (play sleep other)
(rest wake round)

__________ __________

10) (grip catch slap)
(slip clutch caught)

__________ __________

3. Word Link (Homonyms)

In **Word Link** questions two pairs of words are given. A choice of five words is given in the answers. Only one of these words will go equally well with both of these pairs.

Example:

> Which word below will link the two pairs of bracketed words?
>
> **(injure offend)**
> **(coiled looped)**
>
> hurt, smash, straight, wound, twist

1. Scan the answers to see if the word link is obvious.
2. If it is not, think of alternative meanings as these words are homonyms and have more than one meaning.
3. Invent sentences and substitute the words, e.g. 'I can hurt someone' works with the first pair: 'I can **injure**' and 'I can **offend**' but no sentence using 'hurt' will work with **looped** and **coiled**.
4. Continuc this process until the word link is found, e.g. 'I can **injure**' or 'I can **offend**' works with 'I can **wound**'. Also, 'A rope can be **wound**.' It can also be 'coiled' or 'looped.'

The word link for both pairs is: **wound**

Exercise 4: 3 Write the word link for the word pairs:

1) (method way)
(law order)

Possible word links:

road, rule, type,
legal, boss

____

2) (insult snub)
(slim slender)

Possible word links:

grip, slight, thin,
ignore, send

____

3) (leave depart)
(energy drive)

Possible word links:

come, car, go,
exit, verve

____

4) (kit apparatus)
(confront stop)

Possible word links:

give, tackle, tools,
halt, bend

____

5) (subtract minus)
(steal swipe)

Possible word links:

minor, let, take,
steel, hit

____

6) (piece portion)
(fraction area)

Possible word links:

divide, slip, section,
part, zone

____

7) (cash coins)
(switch trade)

Possible word links:

money, sell, change,
buy, purchase

____

8) (level smooth)
(maisonette apartment)

Possible word links:

low, flat, even,
house, caravan

____

© 2012 Stephen Curran

9) (vessel boat)
(art skill)

Possible word links:

craft, ship, paint,
cup, talent

____

10) (lotion ointment)
(elite prime)

Possible word links:

first, salve, sole,
cream, best

____

Score

4. Opposite Meanings (Antonyms)

In these questions it is necessary to find two words, one from each group, that are most **Opposite in Meaning**.

Example: Which two words, one from each bracketed group, are most opposite in meaning?

(agree curse denial)
(swear belief blessing)

1. Scan both sets of words to see if you can spot the answer immediately. If this docs not work move on to step 2.
2. Carefully compare each of the nine possibilities. The answer must be the most opposite in meaning:

   agree - swear; agree - belief; agree - blessing
   curse - swear; curse - belief; **curse - blessing**
   denial - swear; denial - belief; denial - blessing
3. Test out the words in a sentence. They should be the same part of speech and give the opposite meaning, e.g. 'A person can utter a **blessing**', 'A person can utter a **curse**'.

The correct answer is: **curse - blessing**

Exercise 4: 4

Write the words most opposite in meaning:

Score

1) (front up side)
(font back left)

____________ ____________

2) (cheap laze sweet)
(tweet expensive box)

____________ ____________

3) (undo try trick)
(bind double thread)

____________ ____________

4) (climb decent play)
(jump slip descend)

____________ ____________

5) (rich greedy large)
(wealthy poor tasty)

____________ ____________

6) (break take brake)
(pattern make leave)

____________ ____________

7) (conceal control contrast)
(reveal prove change)

____________ ____________

8) (taken gift take)
(gave give grave)

____________ ____________

9) (happy hoping place)
(pleased miserable meal)

____________ ____________

10) (rage range engaged)
(engrossed calm slip)

____________ ____________

5. Odd Ones Out

In these questions, three of the five words are related in some way. Two words are not related to the other three; they are **Odd Ones Out** and must be identified.

Example:

Which two words are the odd ones out?

veal legumes mutton
tubers venison

© 2012 Stephen Curran

1. **Veal**, **mutton** and **venison** can be linked as they are kinds of meat.
2. **Legumes** (seeds and pods) and **tubers** (roots) are both types of vegetables.

The odd ones out are: **legumes** and **tubers**

Exercise 4: 5 Write the odd ones out:

Score

1) fast, slow, speedy, quick, sedate

________ ________

2) star, planet, alien, spirit, moon

________ ________

3) climb, raise, lower, ascend, descend

________ ________

4) frog, newt, bear, cow, dog

________ ________

5) shout, whisper, croak, holler, scream

________ ________

6) biscuit, crisps, cola, water, cake

________ ________

7) pencil, pen, ruler, rubber, crayon

________ ________

8) place, point, gold, position, silver

________ ________

9) envelope, stamp, stomp, letter, packet

________ ________

10) type, write, sort, kind, wrote

________ ________

6. Missing Word

In these questions, the word in capitals has had three consecutive letters removed. These three letters will make one correctly spelt **Missing Word** without changing their order.

© 2012 Stephen Curran

Example: What is the missing three-letter word?

The scholar acquired great **LNING**.

Five possibilities are given in the answers section:

ARE IRE URN EAR ORE

1. Read the sentence carefully and think of the context. This may identify the three-letter word immediately. If this does not work move on to step 2:

2. Space out the letters. Try out the possibilities.

EAR
L NING
(LEARNING)

The correct three-letter word is: **EAR**

Exercise 4: 6 What is the missing three-letter word?

1) The magician made the rabbit **DISAPR**.
The five possibilities are:
PER PIE PEA EAR PEN ______

2) The tourists saw disappointing **WS**.
The five possibilities are:
ARE VIE SET LIE CAR ______

3) The ball went **THER** than expected.
The five possibilities are:
RAT SUN RAN FUR LAT ______

4) He **ATDED** training every Monday and Thursday.
The five possibilities are:
HEN MEN TEN LEN LAN ______

© 2012 Stephen Curran

5) Do not despair - **TE** is still hope!
The five possibilities are:
ARE HEE HER MEN LAD ______

6) The children were looking forward to their **HOAY**.
The five possibilities are:
LAD LID DAD DIN NOD ______

7) The cats that we have as pets are **DOMESTIED**.
The five possibilities are:
DOG PET PAT CAN CAT ______

8) The explorers were **PING** the coastline.
The five possibilities are:
MOP CAP CAT COP MAP ______

9) The robins were **NESG** in the tree.
The five possibilities are:
TAN SIN BIN TIN TON ______

10) The car was **FOLING** the signs for Thorpe Park.
The five possibilities are:
LOW BOW LAW SAW PIN ______

Score

7. Mixed Examples

Exercise 4: 7 Answer the following:

Write the two words that are odd ones out.

1) car, bicycle, house, caravan, bus
______ ______

2) dog, lion, hamster, gorilla, elephant
______ ______

Write the word that will complete the analogy:

3) **Win** is to **lose**
as **succeed** is to
(chose fail rail)

____

4) **More** is to **less**
as **misery** is to
(sadness joy amuse)

____

Write the two words most similar in meaning:

5) (mate enemy foe)
(meat friend meet)

________ ________

Write the two words most opposite in meaning:

6) (select praise need)
(choose repel reject)

________ ________

Write the missing three-letter word:

7) The gardener **CPED** the hedge with shears.

The five possibilities are:
POP RIP LOT LIP ROB ______

8) He watched the sheep **SHING** competition.

The five possibilities are:
EEL EAR ARE APE TEN ______

Write the word link for the pairs of words:

9) (lose colour bleach)
(dim lessen)

Possible word links:
faze, praise, darken,
flue, fade

____

10) (vanish decline)
(diminish die away)

Possible word links:
demean, dwindle,
swindle, leave, lo

____

Score

© 2012 Stephen Curran

Answers

Chapter One

Alphabet Reasoning

Exercise 1: 1a

1) FI
2) MN
3) PU
4) WX
5) DM

Exercise 1: 1b

6) WM
7) OX
8) ND
9) KQ
10) DP

Exercise 1: 2a

1) UT
2) KA
3) LQ
4) JM
5) VR

Exercise 1: 2b

6) IL
7) EG
8) HC
9) IB
10) PQ

Exercise 1: 3

1) WP
2) UV
3) PK
4) AA
5) SK
6) SZ
7) LF
8) HX
9) TU
10) ZA

Exercise 1:4a

1) VW
2) GY
3) AO
4) DG
5) QE

Exercise 1: 4b

6) VJGO
7) SQFOX
8) UGLIQ
9) QYFHN
10) ANLQW

Exercise 1:5a

1) LAP
2) LET
3) WAG
4) VAN
5) CUP

Exercise 1: 5b

6) YFOY
7) YVVH
8) MVVWH
9) DLIP
10) URHS

Exercise 1: 6

1) a) TX b) RS
2) a) PT b) TX
3) a) QN b) RX
4) a) IZ b) SP
5) a) MW b) RK
6) PGEFR
7) KLMRVH
8) CQROX
9) OJXUN
10) KRZML

© 2012 Stephen Curran

Answers

Chapter Two
Word Patterns and Codes

Exercise 2: 1
1) ire
2) lot
3) led
4) pod
5) shop
6) clot
7) fine
8) lion
9) date
10) tab

Exercise 2: 2
1) soar
2) rota
3) late
4) cook
5) tour
6) tape
7) rig
8) tear
9) crane
10) link

Exercise 2: 3
1) 63257
2) 24361
3) 57361
4) CARTS
5) CATCH
6) 57217
7) 24572
8) 12467
9) PEER
10) AGREE

Exercise 2: 4
1) east
2) teal
3) gale
4) step
5) slab
6) mast
7) 73316
8) 53732
9) CLONE
10) SLOPE

Chapter Three
Vocabulary with Spelling

Exercise 3: 1
1) glad and mean (e)
2) plan and trap (t)
3) goat and clove (l)
4) gave and chart (r)
5) crate and beard (e)
6) leap and table (t)
7) rove and nests (s)
8) tend and learn (r)
9) raised and plaid (p)
10) layer and prise (p)

Exercise 3: 2
1) lifetime
2) hammock
3) anybody
4) buttercup
5) goldfish
6) footprint
7) blackboard
8) railroad
9) ringlet
10) careless

Exercise 3: 3
1) method
2) pantry
3) linkage
4) orbit
5) waistcoat
6) bandage
7) grimace
8) handsome
9) knowledge
10) rather

Exercise 3: 4
1) snow
2) play
3) rent
4) wasp
5) crow
6) hand
7) nice
8) yard
9) gram
10) sour

Exercise 3: 5
1) p
2) t
3) n
4) w
5) y
6) k
7) g
8) a
9) m
10) e

© 2012 Stephen Curran

Answers

Exercise 3: 6

1) e
2) o
3) p
4) z
5) a
6) l
7) w
8) c
9) s
10) i

Exercise 3: 7

1) h
2) o
3) p
4) r
5) i
6) a
7) s
8) s
9) b
10) y

Exercise 3: 8

1) font and ramp (r)
2) chip and mall (m)
3) starlight
4) booklet
5) wand
6) twin
7) t
8) r
9) o
10) g

Chapter Four Vocabulary with Meaning

Exercise 4: 1

1) bright
2) see
3) cry
4) fly
5) cold
6) twelve
7) puppy
8) pins
9) foot
10) fought

Exercise 4: 2

1) bucket, pail
2) bread, roll
3) stalk, stem
4) jump, hop
5) neck, throat
6) break, smash
7) woman, lady
8) run, jog
9) sleep, rest
10) grip, clutch

Exercise 4: 3

1) rule
2) slight
3) go
4) tackle
5) take
6) section
7) change
8) flat
9) craft
10) cream

Exercise 4: 4

1) front, back
2) cheap, expensive
3) undo, bind
4) climb, descend
5) rich, poor
6) break, make
7) conceal, reveal
8) take, givc
9) happy, miserable
10) rage, calm

Exercise 4: 5

1) slow, sedate
2) spirit, alien
3) lower, descend
4) frog, newt
5) whisper, croak
6) cola, water
7) ruler, rubber
8) gold, silver
9) stamp, stomp
10) write, wrote

Exercise 4: 6

1) PEA
2) VIE
3) FUR
4) TEN
5) HER
6) LID
7) CAT
8) MAP
9) TIN
10) LOW

© 2012 Stephen Curran

Answers

Exercise 4: 7

1) house, caravan
2) dog, hamster
3) fail
4) joy
5) mate, friend
6) select, reject
7) LIP
8) EAR
9) fade
10) dwindle

© 2012 Stephen Curran

PROGRESS CHARTS

Shade in your score for each exercise on the graph. Add up for your total score. An adult will work out the percentage.

1. ALPHABET REASONING

Scores

10 9 8 7 6 5 4 3 2 1

1 2 3 4 5 6

Exercises

Total Score

Percentage

%

2. WORD PATTERNS AND CODES

Scores

10 9 8 7 6 5 4 3 2 1

1 2 3 4

Exercises

Total Score

Percentage

%

3. VOCABULARY WITH SPELLING

Scores

10 9 8 7 6 5 4 3 2 1

1 2 3 4 5 6 7

Exercises

Total Score

Percentage

%

4. VOCABULARY WITH MEANING

Scores

10 9 8 7 6 5 4 3 2 1

1 2 3 4 5 6 7

Exercises

Total Score

Percentage

%

Add up the percentages and divide by 4

Overall Percentage %

© 2012 Stephen Curran

CERTIFICATE OF

ACHIEVEMENT

This certifies

____

has successfully completed

11+ Verbal Reasoning
Year 4/5 GL & Other Styles
WORKBOOK **1**

Overall percentage score achieved [   ] %

Comment ____________________________________

____

Signed ____________________________________
(teacher/parent/guardian)

Date ____________________________________